Practice Papers

Verbal Reasoning

AGE 9–11

Robin Brown
Chartered Educational Psychologist

This book has been devised to improve your child's performance in selection examinations. It gives you the opportunity to work together towards success in gaining a place at the school of your choice.

Advice on what you can do to help your child is given overleaf. At the centre of the book (pages 15–18) you will find a pull-out section containing answers for each paper. Finally, on page 32 there is a 'Test Profile' to complete to chart your child's progress, together with questions to help your child learn from any mistakes.

ISBN 0 340 72683 0

Text © Robin Brown 1998

The right of Robin Brown to be identified as the author of this work has been asserted by him in accordance with the Copyright, Design and Patents Act 1988.

First published as a W. H. Smith exclusive 1995, this edition published 1998.

All rights reserved. No part of this book may be reproduced, stored in a retrieval system, or transmitted, in any form or by any means, without the prior written permission of the publisher, nor be otherwise circulated in any form of binding or cover other than that in which it is published and without a similar condition being imposed on the subsequent purchaser.

Published by Hodder Children's Books, a division of Hodder Headline plc, 338 Euston Road, London NW1 3BH

Printed and bound in Great Britain

A CIP record is registered by and held at the British Library

The only home learning programme supported by the NCPTA

TIPS FOR PARENTS

- The practice papers within this book offer your child the opportunity to experience questions similar to those that appear in assessment tests around the country. The tests have been designed to give your child an understanding of the principles involved, to develop an ability to reason and to increase self-confidence.

- 'Helpful Hints' are provided at the end of each practice paper. These offer guidance in answering particular types of questions and also recommend valuable study techniques. Encourage your child to cover over this section and only to look at it once the paper has been completed.

- Encourage the development of good exam practice such as:
  - looking over the paper quickly before starting
  - reading the questions carefully and answering exactly what is asked for.
  - answering first the questions that you can answer and then the questions that you find difficult
  - planning your time carefully and working at a steady pace
  - staying calm and doing your best

- Allow 40 minutes for each practice paper.

- Go through the completed paper with your child and read the 'Helpful Hints' that follow. Discuss the 'Test Profile' questions on page 32 and enter the test score on the graph.

- Encourage your child to explain the reasons for giving a particular answer. By explaining the route to an answer, your child's understanding of that type of question will be strengthened and any mistakes will be learnt from. In practice papers such as these, learning how to improve performance is as important as the results in the preparation for future tests.

- Analyse the type of questions your child finds difficult and try to give more practice on these.

- Remember to make the tests enjoyable, to praise successes and to build up your child's confidence.

PRACTICE PAPER 1

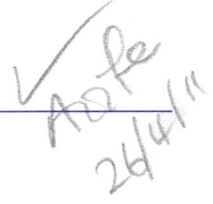

1 Underline the word in each line which does *not* fit in with the rest:

a   tree   banana   grapefruit   pear   grape
b   orange   potato   carrot   turnip   cauliflower
c   car   coach   canoe   bus   lorry
d   Monday   May   Thursday   Saturday   Tuesday
e   kilometre centimetre millimetre   metre   kilogramme
f   cello   violin   viola   double-bass cymbals
g   toe   ankle   elbow   heel   toenail
h   Saturn   Venus   Earth   Mars   Pacific

2 Two words in each line are formed from the same letters. Underline both words. *Allow 1 mark for each pair of correct words.*

a   nest   nail   nets   tents   test   neat
b   sips   hips   pips   shot   ship   pass
c   meals   meats   smile   small   mates
d   shot   hosts   huts   shirt   shut   hits
e   posts   spare   spike   sport   spits   spots
f   woody   stone   works   north   notes   there

3 Mrs Parks visits her mother, Mrs Wood, with her husband and their three children, Liz, John and Laura.

a   How many brothers has Laura?   _____

b   How many children has Mr Parks?   _____

c   How many adults are mentioned?   _____

Underline the correct answer:

d   What relation is John to Mrs Wood?
    son   father   son-in-law   grandson   husband

e   What relation is Mr Parks to Mrs Wood?
    father   husband   son-in-law   grandmother   mother

3

PRACTICE PAPER 1

4 If Asil had 4 more marbles, he would have the same number as Charlotte. Charlotte lives next door to Jane and Jane has half as many marbles as Charlotte. If Jane has 10 marbles, work out how many marbles each child has.

    a Asil   _____

    b Charlotte   _____

    c Jane   _____

5 Underline any words which start and end with the same letter, e.g. *toast*. Allow 1 mark for each correctly identified word.

    a   tiller   tilt   speed   dear   sledge   sisters

    b   rigour   right   queen   pressure   elevate   element

    c   diary   code   did   trust   superior   minimum   barb

6   **a**   Which is the 3rd month of the year?   _____

    b   Which is the month before the 8th month of the year?   _____

    c   Which month has 9 letters in it?   _____

    d   Which month begins with the 6th letter of the alphabet?   _____

    e   Which month ends in a vowel?   _____

7 Write one letter in the box to complete the two words.
e.g. PAR ☐ REE
Putting the letter T in the box gives us the two words, PART and TREE.

    a   HORS ☐ LEPHANT

    b   TRAI ☐ EIGHBOUR

    c   GORG ☐ DGE

    d   MOT ☐ OUSE

    e   LEA ☐ REE

    f   GRAS ☐ EANUT

PRACTICE PAPER 1

8 Underline one word or phrase in each pair of brackets to complete the sentence and make it a true statement.

e.g. A car always has (a sunroof, <u>wheels</u>, legs).

a A girl always has (a hat, a head, shoes).
b A hand always has (a glove, a bag, fingers).
c A donkey always has a (body, saddle, rider).
d Sugar is always (white, brown, sweet).
e The sea is always (blue, wet, cold, warm).
f Coal is always (hot, burning, black, cold).

9 a Which letter comes before the 17th letter in the alphabet? _____

b Make a word from the 15th, 12th and 7th letters of the alphabet. _____

c Make a word from the 1st, 18th, 3rd and 2nd letters of the alphabet. _____

HELPFUL HINTS

3 You could draw a diagram to show the relationships between each person mentioned. Use this to answer the questions.

4 Write down all the names and work out the numbers of marbles from the information given. You would start with Jane as you are told the number of marbles she has. Then consult your list for the answers.

6 Writing the months of the year in order may help you to work out these problems.

8 Make sure you read the question carefully. For example, in **d**, sugar can be white but it is not always white, so 'sweet' is the best answer.

9 You could write out the alphabet. It is easier to find the positions of letters when you have them all in order in front of you.

PRACTICE PAPER 2

1 Underline the word which describes all the other words in the line:

a   apple   banana   fruit   pear   orange
b   blue   colours   brown   yellow   red
c   fish   trout   salmon   cod   plaice
d   sycamore   oak   beech   trees   elm
e   buildings   bungalow   garage   mosque   shops
f   December   March   months   June   September

2
a   What is the 12th letter of the alphabet?
b   Which letter comes before the 9th letter of the alphabet?
c   Which letter comes two places after the 17th letter of the alphabet?
d   Make a word from the 1st, 20th and 2nd letters of the alphabet.
e   Make a word from the 1st, 18th, 13th and 11th letters of the alphabet.
f   Which letter appears twice in CROTCHET but not in CROSSING?

3
a   If today is Tuesday, what day is it the day after tomorrow?
b   If yesterday was Friday, what day is it tomorrow?
c   If tomorrow is Wednesday, what day was it the day before yesterday?

4 Underline the word which has the opposite meaning to the word in capitals:

a   FULL   large   enlarge   empty   fat   big
b   BENT   broad   straight   curved   strong
c   ATTACK   default   deform   defame   defend   defer
d   WEAK   month   day   year   strong   strange
e   QUIET   noon   nostalgic   noiseless   nosey   noisy
f   LOST   last   final   fourth   found   foul

PRACTICE PAPER 2

5 If 594328672 in code means CHRISTMAS,

    a   6728 means _____   b   8436 means _____

    c   26748 means _____   d   67859 means _____

If 75464129 in code means WARDROBE,

    e   6457 means _____   f   2954 means _____

    g   21546 means _____   h   21441796 means _____

6 Complete these analogies:

    a   *Man* is to *boy* as *woman* is to _____

    b   *Cattle* is to *herd* as *sheep* is to _____

    c   *Forest* is to *trees* as *library* is to _____

    d   *Crew* is to *sailors* as *army* is to _____

    e   *Bird* is to *nest* as *horse* is to _____

7 Each week for 3 weeks, Mr Field gave his class a mental arithmetic test. The pupils were given marks out of 20.
Each pupil's marks for the 3 weeks are shown in the table below.

NAME	WEEK 1	WEEK 2	WEEK 3
Peter	14	12	16
Jane	17	8	16
Abdul	15	19	9
Ralph	20	12	17
Parminder	18	18	18

    a   Who scored the most marks in week 2? _____

    b   Who scored the most marks in week 3? _____

    c   Who scored the lowest mark in week 2? _____

    d   Which was Jane's worst week? _____

    e   Who got every question correct in one week? _____

    f   Who had less than half marks in week 3? _____

PRACTICE PAPER 2

    g Who found the test most difficult in week 1? _____

    h Who had the most consistent scores? _____

    i Which was Abdul's best week? _____

8 Unscramble the word in capitals and write the correct word opposite:

    a A DOAR is what cars drive on. _____

    b CHEBE is the name of a tree. _____

    c A MARECS is a piercing cry. _____

    d A NIPICC is an outdoor meal. _____

9 Lynn is 14 years old. Vijay is 1 year older than Jason but 2 years younger than Lynn.

    a How old is Jason? _____

    b Who is the oldest? _____

    c Who is the youngest? _____

HELPFUL HINTS

2 You could write out the alphabet. It is easier to find the positions of letters when you have them all in order in front of you.

3 Writing the days of the week in order may help you to work out these problems.

5 Write the numbers above the letters of CHRISTMAS. It is then quicker to decode the questions.

7 If you find it difficult to understand a question, read it carefully and consider it from different angles. For example, in **g**, the person with the lowest mark is the clue to who found the test most difficult.

9 Write down all the names and work out the ages from the information given. Consult your list for the answers.

PRACTICE PAPER 3

1 Look carefully at the words below. In each line, one word cannot be formed from letters in the word in capitals:

a	HORSESHOE	shore	rose	horn	horse
b	NUMEROUS	some	room	rose	sour
c	TEACHERS	cheers	search	torch	teach	tears
d	DAUGHTER	laugh	dear	rate	thug	heart
e	RECTANGLE	glean	angel	glad	near	reel
f	EDUCATION	eat	cat	die	tin	not	dim
g	CONTEMPORARY	poem	tempo	poets	party	motor

2 If ENTHUSIASM in code is AXCDEFBHFR,

SHAME is _____ and MATHS is _____

FHRA means _____ and RBXECA means _____

3 Complete these analogies by underlining the correct word in the brackets:

a *Up* is to *down* as *first* is to (side, second, last).
b *Pear* is to *fruit* as *potato* is to (soup, vegetable, carrot, orange).
c *Pig* is to *pork* as *cow* is to (beef, lamb, chicken, pie).
d *Mother* is to *daughter* as *father* is to (uncle, nephew, cousin, son).

Now complete these analogies by underlining one word from each pair of brackets. *There is one mark for each correct word.*

e *Month* is to *year* as (stone, hair, day) is to (weed, week, weak).
f *Knee* is to *leg* as (elbow, head, toe) is to (skirt, art, arm).
g *Grass* is to *green* as (coal, wood, leaf) is to (pink, black, sky).
h *Bee* is to *hive* as (lion, dog, lamb) is to (stable, nest, kennel).

PRACTICE PAPER 3

4 Underline the word in each line which is *not* in alphabetical order:

- a   forty   green   left   tooth   gear
- b   alarm   anchor   direct   copy   cure   curl
- c   rock   white   unfair   union   velvet
- d   part   penny   pride   personal   petrol
- e   heavy   hutch   hedge   hero   high

5 Underline the two words that must change place for the sentences to make sense.
e.g. The chef <u>knife</u> the bread with a <u>cut.</u>
There is one mark for each correct word.

- a   The woman put the lock in the key to open the door.
- b   We saw the thunder and heard the lightning during the storm.
- c   When the umbrella started she put up her rain.
- d   The hospital took the injured passengers from the accident to the nearest ambulance.
- e   The teacher class the asked if Cardiff was in Wales or France.

6 Hussein is one year younger than Mark but three years older than Maria. Sarah is Mark's sister and is three years younger than him. Sarah and Maria support the same football team but Hussein watches a rival team in the same league. Mark is 13 years old and does not like football.

- a   How old is Sarah?   _____
- b   How old is Hussein?   _____
- c   How old is Sarah's brother?   _____
- d   Who does not support a football team?   _____
- e   How old is Maria?   _____

PRACTICE PAPER 3

7 Underline the word in the right-hand column which goes with the words in the left-hand column:

a circle   square   octagon   Pluto   rectangle   roll
b Sunday   Monday   Tuesday   November   January   Friday
c birch   oak   ash   maple   beach   arm   popular
d drive   avenue   street   house   flat   lane   tree
e aunt   uncle   father   ant   under   mother   friend
f beef   lamb   chicken   chips   peas   carrots   pork
g Spain   France   Germany   Paris   Berlin   Italy   Rome

HELPFUL HINTS

1 A quick way of doing this is to scan the list and look for any letter in a word which does not appear in the target word, rather than checking each word letter by letter.

2 The questions can be answered more quickly if you write the letters of the code above the letters of ENTHUSIASM. Make sure you read the questions carefully because the first two ask you to write the words *in* code and the last two to work out the word *from* the code.

4 When the first letters of the words are the same, you work out the alphabetical order from the second letter. For example, '*pr*ide' should come after '*pe*trol'.

5 Read the question slowly and listen for the parts which do not make sense. Try changing these words first.

6 You could draw a diagram from the facts you are given and then use this information to answer the questions. Sometimes you have to deduce the answer. For example, for **c**, you are told Sarah is Mark's sister, so it follows that Mark is Sarah's brother and you are given his age as 13 years. For **d**, you are told Mark does not like football so we can assume that he does not support a football team. Also, you are told that Sarah, Maria and Hussein all support football teams.

PRACTICE PAPER 4

1 Underline the word which describes the home of the animal in capitals:

a	BEE	burrow	hive	tree	stable	den
b	PIG	nest	hive	home	house	sty
c	SNAIL	kennel	cocoon	shell	nest	sty
d	DOG	box	hive	cage	kennel	tree
e	RABBIT	stable	nest	sty	hutch	kennel
f	LION	set	holt	lodge	den	cell

2 Sara is taller than Ben and Joe, and Alan is taller than Sara. Ben is taller than Joe.

a Who is the shortest? _____

b Who is the tallest? _____

3 School will be closed tomorrow. Today is a day in which the letter E occurs twice.

a What day is school closed? _____

b What day was it yesterday? _____

4 Look carefully at the words below. In each line, one word cannot be formed from letters in the word in capitals. Underline this word:

a	MULTIPLY	tip	pit	top	lip	
b	INFANT	fat	in	nit	not	an
c	MARKET	mat	team	tar	rate	rock
d	HISTORICAL	roast	stair	rat	rot	shore
e	HIPPOPOTAMUS	pot	pop	mat	meat	shop	ship
f	HANDKERCHIEF	chief	hand	chair	drink	drunk

12

PRACTICE PAPER 4

5 Underline one word in each pair of brackets so that the passage makes sense. *Allow 1 mark for each correct answer.*

It was two weeks (after, during, before) Christmas and the children were getting excited. They were looking forward to performing in the school (baths, concert, magazine) and Jennifer had been chosen to (sing, eat, hop) a solo in the grand finale. At home they were busy making (decisions, decorations, trouble) out of crêpe paper and helping Dad put the Christmas tree (down, under, up) whilst Mum checked the (flowers, paper, bulbs) in the lights. By evening, the house looked pretty and the children talked with eager (anticipation, anxiety, analysis) about the presents they hoped to receive.

6 Underline the longest word in each line:

a hospital   hostage   hostile   house   helicopter
b committee   companion   commissioner   commodore
c temperature   tendency   telescope   technical
d thousand   threshold   threaten   Thursday
e negative   neighbour   nervous   neglect   narrate
f laughter   lawyer   latitude   laboratory
g juvenile   junction   justice   jungle   jubilation

7 Mrs Barnes lives with her husband and two children, Elaine and Jonathan, next door to her sister, Mrs Miles. Mrs Miles also has two children, Ann and Jeremy.

a What relation is Mrs Miles to Mrs Barnes?
   aunt   uncle   sister   sister-in-law

b What relation is Mrs Miles to Elaine?
   mother   daughter   aunt   grandmother   niece

c What relation is Mr Barnes to Jonathan?
   son   father   uncle   grandfather   nephew

PRACTICE PAPER 4

d What relation is Mr Barnes to Mrs Miles?
uncle   father-in-law   grandfather   brother-in-law

e What relation is Jonathan to Elaine?
cousin   uncle   sister   brother   brother-in-law

f What relation is Ann to Jonathan?
cousin   aunt   sister   sister-in-law   mother

8 Elizabeth is 10 years old. She is 2 years older than her sister, Angela, and twice as old as her brother, Ian.

a How old is Ian? _____

b How old is Angela? _____

c Who is the youngest? _____

9 Below is a timetable of the trains leaving Londis to various destinations.

Londis to	Leaves Londis	Arrives
Pardiff	9.00 a.m.	9.55 a.m.
Meeds	9.40 a.m.	10.15 a.m.
Glasgon	9.05 a.m.	9.30 a.m.

a How long does it take to travel from Londis to Glasgon? _____

b How long does it take to travel from Londis to Pardiff? _____

c How long does the journey from Londis to Meeds take? _____

d Which is the shortest journey? _____

e If my bus is late and gets into Londis railway station at 9.10 a.m., can I still catch the train to Meeds? _____

ANSWERS

PRACTICE PAPER 1

1 a tree **b** orange **c** canoe
  d May **e** kilogramme
  f cymbals **g** elbow **h** Pacific

2 *1 mark for each correct pair of words:*
  a nest/nets **b** ship/hips
  c meats/mates **d** huts/shut
  e post/spots **f** stone/notes

3 a 1 brother **b** 3 children
  c 3 adults **d** grandson
  e son-in-law

4 a 16 **b** 20 **c** 10

5 *1 mark for each word:*
  a tilt, sisters **b** rigour, elevate
  c did, trust, minimum, barb

6 a March **b** July **c** September
  d February **e** June

7 a E **b** N **c** E
  d H **e** F **f** P

8 a head **b** fingers **c** body
  d sweet **e** wet **f** black

9 a P **b** log **c** crab

PRACTICE PAPER 2

1 a fruit **b** colours **c** fish
  d trees **e** buildings
  f months

2 a L **b** H **c** S
  d BAT or TAB **e** MARK **f** T

3 a Thursday **b** Sunday
  c Sunday

4 a empty **b** straight **c** defend
  d strong **e** noisy **f** found

5 a MAST **b** TRIM **c** SMART
  d MATCH **e** DRAW **f** BEAR
  g BOARD **h** BORROWED

6 a girl **b** flock **c** books
  d soldiers **e** stable

7 a Abdul **b** Parminder **c** Jane
  d week 2 **e** Ralph **f** Abdul
  g Peter **h** Parminder
  i week 2

8 a road **b** beech **c** scream
  d picnic

9 a 11 years **b** Lynn **c** Jason

ANSWERS

PRACTICE PAPER 3

1. **a** horn **b** room **c** torch
   d laugh **e** glad **f** dim
   g poets
2. *1 mark for each correct answer:*
   FDHRA RHCDF SAME
   MINUTE
3. **a** last **b** vegetable **c** beef
   d son
   1 mark for each correct word:
   e day, week **f** elbow, arm
   g coal, black **h** dog, kennel
4. **a** gear **b** direct **c** white
   d pride **e** hutch
5. *1 mark for each correct word:*
   a lock, key **b** saw, heard
   c umbrella, rain
   d hospital, ambulance
   e class, asked
6. **a** 10 years **b** 12 years
   c 13 years (Mark) **d** Mark
   e 9 years
7. **a** rectangle **b** Friday **c** maple
   d lane **e** mother **f** pork
   g Italy

PRACTICE PAPER 4

1. **a** hive **b** sty **c** shell
   d kennel **e** hutch **f** den
2. **a** Joe **b** Alan
3. **a** Thursday **b** Tuesday
4. **a** top **b** not **c** rock
   d shore **e** meat **f** drunk
5. *1 mark for each correct answer:*
   before, concert, sing, decorations,
   up, bulbs, anticipation
6. **a** helicopter **b** commissioner
   c temperature **d** threshold
   e neighbour **f** laboratory
   g jubilation
7. **a** sister **b** aunt **c** father
   d brother-in-law **e** brother
   f cousin
8. **a** 5 years **b** 8 years **c** Ian
9. **a** 25 minutes **b** 55 minutes
   c 35 minutes
   d Londis to Glasgon **e** Yes
10. **a** heron **b** rugby **c** oar
    d cake **e** herring **f** sand

ANSWERS

PRACTICE PAPER 5

1 *1 mark for each correct pair of words:*
  a sun, son   **b** chair, pair
  c heard, herd   **d** wood, could
  e heart, chart   **f** rows, rose
2 a feet   **b** paw   **c** eight
  d rose   **e** tears   **f** oar
3 a 8 years   **b** 13 years
  c Mustapha
4 a Susie   **b** 9 years   **c** 7 years
  d 2 years
5 a 8   **b** 11   **c** 24   **d** 11
  e 6   **f** 27   **g** 3
6 *1 mark for each correct answer:*
  1 Yasmin   2 Charlotte   3 Nick
  4 Ayse
7 a waste   **b** sore   **c** night
  d cereal   **e** read   **f** wait
8 a son   **b** brother   **c** daughter
  d grandmother   **e** husband
  f son   **g** sister
9 a behind   **b** forget   **c** inside
  d newspaper   **e** breakfast
  f upset   **g** grandfather

PRACTICE PAPER 6

1 a RATE   **b** ART
2 a YES   **b** CURE   **c** RESCUE
3 a XSMZ   **b** XBMMS
  c SMBAX
4 a 32   **b** 7.25 p.m.   **c** 5 days
  d 7.24 a.m.   **e** 12 children
5 a 10 years   **b** 8 years
  c 5 years
6 *1 mark for each correct answer:*
  sail, blew, see, beach, too, knew, currents
7 a 1450   **b** 1539   **c** 1917
  d 1699   **e** 1508
8 a Saturday   **b** Mike   **c** Gillian
  d Joanne
9 a LION   **b** DOG   **c** GIRAFFE
  d BEAR   **e** RAT   **f** TIGER
  g CAT   **h** ZEBRA   **i** CHICKEN
  j RABBIT
10 a feeble   **b** tough   **c** interior
  d broad   **e** unhappy   **f** old
  g eat   **h** leave

ANSWERS

PRACTICE PAPER 7

1. **a** 321　**b** 8657　**c** elephant
   d cathedral　**e** 9738
2. **a** white　**b** fur　**c** 6　**d** 12
   e 6
3. **a** h<u>o</u>tel　**b** fl<u>o</u>wer　**c** au<u>th</u>or
   d r<u>e</u>f<u>e</u>ree　**e** pa<u>dd</u>le　**f** w<u>h</u>i<u>s</u>tle
4. **a** TRAP　**b** PARROT
   c ARMOUR
5. **a** August　**b** September
   c June　**d** May and September
   e August to September
   f May and July　**g** May
6. **a** park　**b** teacher
   c rose or sore　**d** cart　**e** door
7. **a** Z　**b** A　**c** N
8. **a** Beth　**b** Liz　**c** Ralph
   d Liz　**e** Ralph
9. *1 mark for each correct answer:*
   1 Gordon　2 Sharon　3 Kate　4 Peter
10. **a** 5678　**b** 0.003　**c** minute
    d pond　**e** ant　**f** 10%
    g 5+1

PRACTICE PAPER 8

1. **a** 8　**b** 9　**c** 55　**d** 37
   e 20　**f** B　**g** ST　**h** NPO
   i DC　**j** G7
2. **a** H　**b** T　**c** A　**d** H
   e D　**f** Y
3. *1 mark for each correct answer:*
   into　pressed　down　met
   leaving　catch　station　checked
   saw　depart
4. **a** bus station　**b** newsagent
   c railway station　**d** garage
   e bus station　**f** No　**g** Yes
   h Yes　**i** Yes
5. **a** Joy　**b** Joy
   c Ann and Mustapha　**d** 15
   e 52
6. **a** 10 years　**b** 9 years
   c 8 years　**d** Abdul
7. **a** bad　**b** expensive　**c** weak
   d front　**e** rude　**f** sell

PRACTICE PAPER 4

10 Underline the odd word out in each line:

- a plaice   cod   halibut   hake   heron   herring
- b chess   draughts   rugby   dominoes   cards
- c oak   elm   oar   ash   yew   beech
- d tea   cake   coffee   lemonade   orange juice
- e cuckoo   kingfisher   heron   herring   raven
- f sea   sand   river   stream   lake

HELPFUL HINTS

2 You could use the information to make a list, with the name of the tallest person at the top. Use this list to help you answer the questions.

4 Try scanning the line quickly to look for any letter which does not appear in the target word. If you find this difficult, you could tick off the letters in the target word as you check each word in the line, but this is not the quickest method.

5 If you cannot decide which word fits, read on and come back to it. Information you are given later in the passage may help you to decide which word to choose.

7 If you find this type of question difficult, you could draw a diagram to show who is related to who and use this information to help you answer the questions.

PRACTICE PAPER 5

1   Underline the two words in a line which rhyme with each other.
Allow 1 mark for each correct pair of rhyming words.

   a   sum   sun   sit   sat   son   sort   soon

   b   chair   chore   park   pair   port   motor

   c   hard   heard   hide   half   herd   hold

   d   wood   word   sword   called   could   catch

   e   hard   heart   meat   meal   mute   chart

   f   road   ride   rows   rails   rise   rose   reeds

2   The missing word in each line rhymes with the word in capitals.
   e.g. LESS   A game.   *Chess*

   a   MEAT   Attached to your leg.   _____

   b   DOOR   Attached to the leg of a dog.   _____

   c   MATE   A number.   _____

   d   MOWS   A flower.   _____

   e   CHEERS   Crying.   _____

   f   FLOOR   In a rowing boat.   _____

3   Mustapha is 5 years older than Jane and Jane is 3 years younger than Gill. Gill is 11 years old.

   a   How old is Jane?   _____

   b   How old is Mustapha?   _____

   c   Who is the oldest?   _____

4   Nizam will be 8 years old on his next birthday. Susie was 7 years old 2 years ago.

   a   Who is the oldest now?   _____

   b   How old is Susie now?   _____

   c   How old is Nizam now?   _____

   d   What is the difference in their ages now?   _____

PRACTICE PAPER 5

5 Each of these number sequences follows a regular pattern.
Work out the pattern and fill in the missing number:

a   4   6   ☐   10   12   14   _____
b   3   7   ☐   15   19   23   _____
c   30   27   ☐   21   18   _____
d   2   4   7   ☐   16   22   _____
e   3   ☐   12   24   48   _____
f   37   32   ☐   22   17   _____
g   2   ☐   5   8   12   17   _____

6 In the line to go into school, Nick is behind Charlotte but in front of Ayse. Yasmin is ahead of Charlotte. Use this information to work out the order of the children in the line.
Allow 1 mark for each correct answer.

FRONT
OF THE   1 _____   2 _____   3 _____   4 _____
LINE

7 Underline the correct word in each pair of brackets:

a   Ahmed was careful not to (waste, waist) anything.
b   The girl had a painful (saw, sore) on her leg.
c   It was a dark (night, knight) so it was difficult to see.
d   I always eat (cereal, serial) for breakfast.
e   I like to (reed, read) a book when I go to bed.
f   I had to (wait, weight) for the next bus.

8 Mrs Burns visits her mother, Mrs Dales, with her husband, Peter, and their three children, Jean, Rick and James.

a   What relation is James to Mrs Burns?
    mother   uncle   father   cousin   son   husband
b   What relation is Rick to Jean?
    cousin   sister   brother   father   grandfather

PRACTICE PAPER 5

c What relation is Mrs Burns to Mrs Dales?
daughter   mother   aunt   grandmother   niece

d What relation is Mrs Dales to Jean?
daughter   mother   aunt   grandmother   niece

e What relation is Peter to Mrs Burns?
son   uncle   cousin   husband   father   nephew

f What relation is Rick to Peter?
father   son   uncle   grandfather   brother

g What relation is Jean to James?
mother   brother   sister   aunt   grandmother

9 Underline one word in each set which when put together make a new word without changing the order of the letters. The word from the set on the left always comes first.

e.g. (<u>be</u> at for)   (high <u>low</u> dog)   *below*

a (at be land)   (hind hard high)   _____

b (fight for am)   (guard by get)   _____

c (in lit try)   (sea side sought)   _____

d (old news side)   (port part paper)   _____

e (brake break bring)   (fast slow long)   _____

f (down side up)   (down sort set)   _____

g (aunt mother grand)   (farther father further)   _____

HELPFUL HINTS

3 You are given one person's age so use this to work out the ages of the other people from the information provided.

4 If Nizam will be 8 years old on his next birthday, he must be 7 now. If Susie was 7 years old 2 years ago, she must be 7 + 2 years now, which is 9 years old.

8 Make sure you read the question carefully and give the answer that is asked for. For example, in **a**, James is the son of Mrs Burns and Mrs Burns is the mother of James. Although both 'mother' and 'son' are options in the answer, the question asks for the relation of James to Mrs Burns so you should underline 'son'.

PRACTICE PAPER 6

1 If GREAT in code is XLYZP,

    a LZPY means _____

    b ZLP means _____

2 If SECURITY in code is BMSPXZAO,

    a OMB means _____

    b SPXM means _____

    c XMBSPM means _____

3 If TELESCOPE in code is ZABAXFMSA,

    a SPOT is _____

    b SLOOP is _____

    c POLES is _____

4   **a** The number of my house is twice the number you get when you add 7 to 9. What is the number of my house? _____

    b If my favourite television programme begins at 6.40 p.m. and lasts 45 minutes, when does it finish? _____

    c My birthday is on 4th October. My sister's birthday is on 29th September. How many days before my birthday is my sister's birthday? _____

    d The kitchen clock is 3 minutes fast. If it shows 27 minutes past seven at breakfast, what is the correct time? _____

    e Out of a class of 32, 13 stayed in school and the rest went to a concert. 4 children travelled in Mrs Holt's car, 3 in Mr Tagg's car and the others went in the school minibus. How many children travelled in the minibus? _____

PRACTICE PAPER 6

5 Ryan is half as old as Ann and 3 years younger than Steve. Ann will have to wait 2 years before she is 12 years old.

    a How old is Ann now? _____

    b How old is Steve? _____

    c How old is Ryan? _____

6 Homonyms are words that sound the same but have different spellings and meanings. Underline the correct word in the brackets. *There is 1 mark for each correct answer.*

The sailor raised the (sale, sail) on his yacht as the wind (blue, blew) across the channel. He could not (sea, see) the (beach, beech) as he was (two, too) far out, but he (knew, new) that the wind and strong (currants, currents) would soon help him to reach land.

7 Which year is

    a 1 year after 1449?   (1349   1549   1450   1448)

    b 100 years before 1639?   (1539   1439   1739   1629   1729)

    c 50 years before 1967?   (2017   1927   1937   1947   1917)

    d 2 years before 1701?   (1703   1705   1702   1691   1699)

    e 50 years after 1458?   (1408   1508   1958   1428   1498)

8   **a** I had a party yesterday. Today is a day in which the letters N and U both occur. On what day did I have my party? _____

Joanne arrived at the party before Gillian but after Mike.

    b Who arrived first? _____

    c Who arrived last? _____

Gillian ate more than Mike at the party but not as much as Joanne.

    d Who ate the most? _____

PRACTICE PAPER 6

9 Below are the jumbled names of ten animals. Rearrange the letters and write the names of the animals in the spaces:

a	NLOI	_____	f	GRITE	_____
b	OGD	_____	g	TAC	_____
c	RAFGIFE	_____	h	AZBRE	_____
d	RABE	_____	i	KCCIEHN	_____
e	TAR	_____	j	BBARIT	_____

10 Underline the word in each line which means the same, or is similar in meaning, to the first word in capitals:

a	WEAK	day	week	strong	feeble	powerful
b	HARD	soft	heard	tough	squashy	tender
c	INSIDE	outdoors	exterior	interior	outside	
d	WIDE	big	high	shallow	narrow	broad
e	SAD	unhappy	joyful	happy	laughter	said
f	ANTIQUE	pleasant	beautiful	old	new	young
g	CONSUME	run	east	chase	provide	eat
h	DEPART	leave	arrive	pursue	enter	receive

HELPFUL HINTS

1–3 The questions can be answered quickly if you write the letters of the code above the given word.

4 Follow the instructions carefully. For example, in **a**, 7 + 9 is 16, so twice this number is 16 x 2 = 32, which is the number of the house.

4c Remember, there are only 30 days in September. Count on from 29th September to 4th October, which is 5 days.

4d If the clock is 3 minutes fast, the correct time is 7 hours 27 minutes minus 3 minutes, which is 7.24. If it is breakfast time, it must be in the morning so it is 7.24 a.m.

5 If Ann has to wait 2 years before she is 12 years old, she is 12 – 2 which is 10 years old *now*. You can use this information to work out Ryan's age (half of 10 which is 5 years old). If Ryan is 3 years younger than Steve, Steve must be 3 years older, so he is 5 + 3 years = 8 years old.

6 If you cannot decide which word fits, read on and come back to it. Information you are given later in the passage may help you to decide which word to choose.

PRACTICE PAPER 7

1 Underline the largest in each line:

    a   123   231   312   213   321   132

    b   5678   6785   8567   7856   8657

    c   dog   goat   elephant   cat   mouse

    d   bedroom   kitchen   cathedral   cupboard   bathroom

    e   7893   8937   8973   9738   3897

2 Complete these analogies by underlining the correct answer in the brackets:

    a   *Grass* is to *green* as *snow* is to (black, purple, white).

    b   *Tree* is to *leaf* as *rabbit* is to (feathers, fur, scales).

    c   *2* is to *4* as *3* is to (4, 2, 6).

    d   *5* is to *15* as *4* is to (16, 12, 8).

    e   *24* is to *8* as *18* is to (16, 26, 6).

3 Read the clues and fill in the missing letters:

    a   ___otel   Guests pay to stay here.

    b   ___l___wer   Blossom on a plant.

    c   Au___ ___or   A person who writes books.

    d   ___ef___r___e   An umpire or judge.

    e   P___d___le   A small oar on a boat.

    f   W___is___l___   To blow through your lips and produce a shrill sound.

4 If 123245678 in code is PARAMOUNT,

    a   8321 means   _____

    b   123358 means   _____

    c   234563 means   _____

PRACTICE PAPER 7

5 The chart gives information about the weather on the tropical island of Dowlais. Use this information to answer the questions below.

MONTH	Average day temperature	Average hours of sunshine	Average monthly rainfall
May	23°C	6	16 cm
June	26°C	7	19 cm
July	29°C	8.5	16 cm
August	31°C	9	25 cm
September	28°C	6	48 cm

a   Which month has the highest daytime temperature? _____

b   Which is the wettest month? _____

c   Which month has an average monthly rainfall of 19 cm? _____

d   Which two months have the same average hours of sunshine? _____

e   The biggest difference in rainfall from one month to the next is?   from _____ to _____

f   Which two months have the same average rainfall? _____

g   Which is the coolest month? _____

6 Each clue below refers to the position of a letter in the alphabet. Rearrange the letters to work out what each word is:

a   16th, 1st, 11th, 18th.   _____

b   5th, 18th, 20th, 5th, 1st, 3rd, 8th.   _____

c   18th, 19th, 15th, 5th.   _____

d   20th, 18th, 3rd, 1st.   _____

e   15th, 15th, 18th, 4th.   _____

7 a   Which letter occurs once in MARZIPAN and once in ZOOLOGY?   _____

b   Which letter occurs twice in STAGNANT and once in SPARE?   _____

c   Which letter is in SPEND but not in SPEED?   _____

PRACTICE PAPER 7

8 Liz was wearing a white blouse with a blue skirt and white socks.
Ralph wore his favourite white T-shirt, black cap and trainers.
Beth came to the park in her boots, blue jeans and green T-shirt.

   a Who was wearing boots? _____
   b Who was wearing both white and blue? _____
   c Who was wearing a hat? _____
   d Who was not wearing a T-shirt? _____
   e Who was not wearing anything blue or green? _____

9 In the queue for dinner, Sharon and Kate are behind Gordon but in front of Peter. Kate is behind Sharon. Work out the order of the children in the queue.
There is 1 mark for each correct answer.

FRONT OF THE QUEUE   **1** _____   **2** _____   **3** _____   **4** _____

10 Underline the smallest in each line:

   a   5678   6785   7865   5867   8765
   b   0.03   0.003   0.3   3.0   0.1
   c   week   month   minute   year   hour   day
   d   ocean   pond   river   lake   sea
   e   whale   man   tiger   ant   woman   giraffe
   f   10%   15%   95%   20%   25%   69%
   g   2 + 5   6 + 1   8 + 7   5 + 1   3 + 4

HELPFUL HINTS

2 You get 15 by multiplying 5 by 3. If you multiply 4 by 3 (4 x 3), the answer is 12.

4 The questions can be answered quickly if you write the code numbers above the given word.

5 Make sure that your answers are exactly what is asked for.

For example, two months have the same average hours of sunshine but, in **f**, you are actually asked which two months have the same average rainfall.

8 You can answer the questions quickly if you make a list of the clothes each person is wearing.

PRACTICE PAPER 8

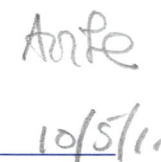

1 Each sequence below follows a pattern. Work out the pattern and fill in the missing numbers or letters:

a 2   4   6   ☐   10   12   _____
b 1   3   5   7   ☐   11   13   _____
c 22   33   44   ☐   66   77   88   _____
d 49   46   43   40   ☐   34   31   _____
e 80   40   ☐   10   5   _____
f E   D   C   ☐   A   _____
g MN   OP   QR   ☐   UV   WX   _____
h BDC   EGF   HJI   KML   ☐   QSR   _____
i JI   HG   FE   ☐   BA   _____
j D4   E5   F6   ☐   H8   I9   _____

2 Write one letter in the box to complete the first word and begin the second:

a MOT ☐ OSE   b PA ☐ AR
c SE ☐ NGLE   d AS ☐ AZARD
e FOL ☐ OOR   f EAS ☐ AWN

3 Underline one word in each pair of brackets so that the passage makes sense. *Allow 1 mark for each correct answer.*

Ted stepped (under, into) the lift and (pressed, picked) the button to take him (up, on to, down) from the sixth floor to the ground floor. He (met, may) his friends Peter and Maria before (jumping, leaving, catching) the flats to (catch, throw) the bus to the railway (station, engine, airport). They (wrote, checked) the timetable and (tasted, saw, touched) that their train was due to (demand, depart, depend) at 09.15.

29

PRACTICE PAPER 8

4 Underline the correct answers:

```
┌─────────────────────────────────────────────────────────┐
│   BUS STATION                           POST OFFICE     │
│              BEECH STREET                               │
│         ┌─A─┐                          ┌─GARAGE─┐       │
│  BAKERY │ S │   ┌─NEWS-─┐                               │
│         │ H │   │ AGENT │                               │
│  HIGH STREET A                          RAILWAY         │
│         │ V │                           STATION         │
│  BUTCHER│ E │                                           │
│         │ N │                                           │
│         │ U │                                           │
│         │ E │                                           │
│              STATION ROAD                               │
└─────────────────────────────────────────────────────────┘
```

- **a** Which of these is in Beech Street?
  bakery   butcher   bus station   railway station
- **b** Which of these is in Ash Avenue?
  bakery   newsagent   butcher   railway station
- **c** Which of these is not in Beech Street?
  bus station   garage   railway station   post office
- **d** Which is nearest to the post office?
  garage   bakery   butcher   railway station
- **e** Which is furthest from the railway station?
  bakery   butcher   bus station   newsagent
- **f** Can you buy meat in the High Street?   YES / NO
- **g** Can you buy a magazine in Ash Avenue?   YES / NO
- **h** Can you buy petrol in Beech Street?   YES / NO
- **i** Could I catch a train from Station Road?   YES / NO

5 Richard had 11 sweets, Ann had one less than Richard, Joy had 14 and Lucy had 7. Mustapha counted his and found that he had 10 sweets.

- **a** Who had the most sweets? _____
- **b** Who had twice as many sweets as Lucy? _____
- **c** Which two children had the same number of sweets? _____

PRACTICE PAPER 8

   d If Ann gave half her sweets to Mustapha, how many would he have then? _____

   e How many sweets did the children have altogether? _____

6 Abdul was 8 years old 2 years ago. His friend, Lesley, is 2 years younger than him and Wendy is 1 year older than Lesley.

   a How old is Abdul now? _____

   b How old is Wendy now? _____

   c How old is Lesley now? _____

   d Who will be the oldest in five years' time? _____

7 Underline the word which has the opposite meaning to the word in capitals:

a	GOOD	kind	deep	bad	polite	bat
b	CHEAP	bold	expensive	experience	economical	
c	STRONG	mighty	week	weak	stout	tough
d	BACK	frontier	tail	front	dorsal	rear
e	POLITE	right	noble	nice	normal	rude	wrong
f	PURCHASE	acquire	sell	procure	obtain	buy

HELPFUL HINTS

3 If you cannot decide which word fits, read on and come back to it. Information you are given later may help you to work out the correct answer. For example, if Ted went from the sixth floor to the ground floor he must have 'pressed the button to take him *down*' in the lift.

4 You have to make deductions from the map. For example, the answer to **h** is 'Yes' because there is a garage in Beech Street so you can buy petrol there.

6 Work out Abdul's age first. If Abdul was 8 years old 2 years ago, he must be 8+2 = 10 years old now. Use this information to work out Lesley's age, then work out Wendy's age as she is one year older than Lesley. In **d**, Abdul is the oldest now so he will still be the oldest in 5 years' time.

TEST PROFILE

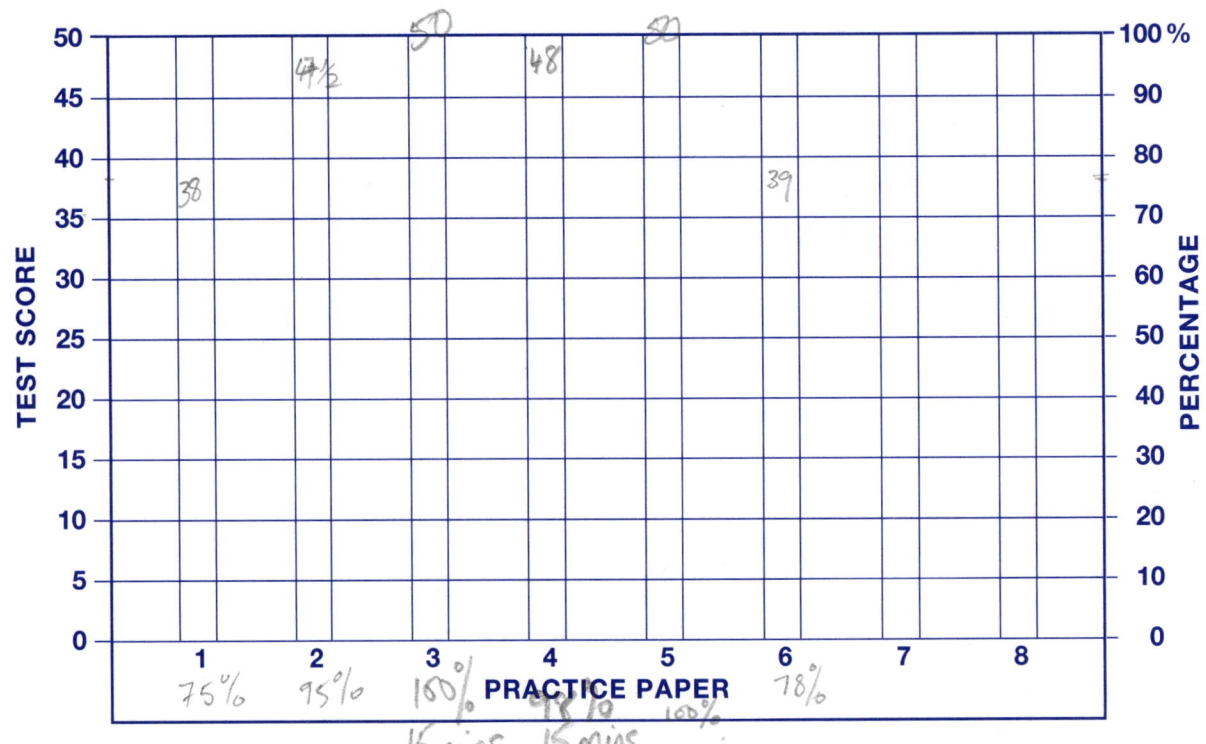

You can chart your progress on this graph. Find your score on the left of the graph and then put a cross in the appropriate column. The right-hand side of the chart converts your score to a percentage (a score out of 100).

Look at the pattern of your progress and ask yourself some questions:

- Are there some types of questions at which you are better and some which you find difficult?
- Which type of questions should you practise more of?
- Did you read the questions carefully?
- Did you misinterpret any questions?
- Did you answer exactly what was asked for?
- Did you forget how to do some questions?
- If you made a mistake on a question, do you know where you went wrong?
- Did you run out of time?

By answering questions like these you can learn about yourself and pick up clues about how you can improve.